THE LINDBERGH HALF-CENTURY

In memory of my mother, Alice Miller Lietz,
and my father, Robert John Lietz, Sr.,
and for my sister.

THE LINDBERGH HALF-CENTURY

POETRY BY
ROBERT LIETZ

L'EPERVIER
PRESS

ACKNOWLEDGMENTS

Some of the poems in this book have been published in the following journals: *Chariton Review, Epoch, Ironwood, The Literary Review, Manhattan Poetry Review, Mid-American Review, The Missouri Review, The Montana Review, The Ontario Review, Oxford Magazine, Porch, Quarterly West, Sou'wester, Sun Dog, Tendril, Willow Springs.*

Some of the poems in *The Lindbergh Half-Century* are dedicated as follows "Marshfield, the Atlantic: 1938; Palermo, Upstate New York: 1976," *to Dick Fitts and Tom Dunn.* "Sundays in Parish Neighborhoods," *to my uncles, Andrew Egle and Harold Raleigh.* "First Confessions," *to Kevin Dombroske.* "Homecoming," *to Fred Muratori.* "Married Mother Out of Her Profession," *to William Forrest.* "Turncoat," *to Anthony Hecht.* "In a Late Hour," *to Charles Heppeler, Sr.* "The Lindbergh Half-Century," *to Albert Goldbarth.* "Night Swimming Outside Ithaca," *to Cecil Giscombe and Kathy Wright.* "Montreal, after Two Rains," *to Walt and Barbara Dubiel.* "Thanksgiving Weekend: the Last Touch Football for the Twenty-fifth Season," *to Mike Bergett.* "For Matthew Clarkson, for Luke Moore Clarkson (In Memoriam)," *to Barbara Moore Clarkson.*

Library of Congress Cataloging-in-Publication Data

Lietz, Robert.
The Lindbergh half-century.

Poems.
I. Title.
PS3562.I4534L5 1986 811'.54 86-3558
ISBN 0-934332-47-9

Book Design by Bridget Culligan
Cover Art by David Reif

The publication of this book was made with a grant from the National Endowment for the Arts, a Federal agency.

L'Epervier Press books are distributed by: Bookslinger, 213 Fourth Street, Saint Paul, Minnesota, 55101, and Small Press Distribution, 1784 Shattuck Avenue, Berkeley, California, 94709.

L'Epervier Press

CONTENTS

THE LINDBERGH HALF-CENTURY

AFTER SLEDDING

IN FLOOD COUNTRY

Marshfield, the Atlantic: 1938;
Palermo, Upstate New York: 1976

The house stood up to storm, like a cramp
the storm could not stomp out.
Families wintered at their risk. Some nights
were wicker chairs and shoulders,

some irreverence talked out. But nobody
came for cards that year. There was nothing
for the scrapbooks save a cousin's
muddy drowning, and years back the skin

a cousin's hammer opened. The next year,
too hot to swim even. But the roof held out,
held up anyway in winter. Listen, at thirty
I expected history. At thirty

I could have killed them all, thinned
that summer crowd by one. And at thirty
still vivid, old Doc Hemmer in his hunting jacket
sewing a boy's scalp. I remembered

sounds, the dim ceiling light, that needle
closing skin, the hurt I heard
but could not feel. That house still standing
over salt-ground stone, and flagstones,

weed-angled stones impossible in winter,
leading down from the front stoop
to stairs up to the seawall, and bonfires
beyond that wall still warm

from the day's heat: I missed that attitude
altogether, the bonfire and moon-illumined summer,
the girl beyond the seawall with her palm
raised up to stars. Tonight, inland

under stars, I walk over these few acres
from the wood I notched and fit.
Barnswallows dip, over water, over uncut grass,
and irregular jots that might have

been birds once smudge air at further distance.
After the cicadas' gossip
last light can mean all sorts of the same thing:
a hearsay gotten by, bankruptcy,

stock-jarred bone. And indoors after dark,
recalled by netted ceiling in a parlor
hundreds of miles inland, their faces clear,
reminders of salt water, backsides

of wood coins the old men around plain tables
spent their lives on not to show us.

Diorama: The Late Fifties

A spring window raised. Curtains airing
in the light wind. A song from the Forties
stops him, boy taking the shortcut to the park
between the houses. 1959, the glare
of Hiroshima dulled, a kind of conciliation
with high whine. And to drown that, men push
their power mowers through spare grass,
heavy men regard their attenuated shadows.
The boy crouches behind the clipped hedge-row,
believes she does not see him, the woman
cleaning her opened windows from inside. The War
was not hers, not his, nor his, husband
resolved to be more cautious about his diet,
nor the smudge of ideologies the local press
stirs up. He regards the thumb he scalded,
figure on the edge of fresh cut grass, the faint
scar left after the blister split and healed,
the mark of the world on him as he fears,
unconsciously humming the standard he woke up to.
Wind this morning blew the puddles dry,
at the same time threatening more rain, left
this mixed olive green and sunlight, cast
on a woman's cheek and forearm, this lighter wind
and freight of orange and yellow petals.
She steps down the backsteps to the hammock
where a sunburned man is resting. They will
learn to quarrel right, to slice the Gruyere
and provolone they have not yet learned to savor.
And the boy will call them back, but later,
seeing the drab figure of a gunner in the pocket
of an old mitt, the leather worn, webbing
ripped through, boy born in the mid-Forties. . .

Pebbles rolling down a slide, a punt,
or the quiet spreading through a park
after the cutters have shut down, the cicadas
filling up that quiet first, they recall
that summer, a boy quickening like invention,
and their voices, distracting him
from a song he almost sings to,
contributing his bit.

Middle October

Four seasons overlap. A single window
gathers leaf-must. There is no comfort
in the day moon, faint as the contrails
blown across its face, nor in the city's
blameless mirrors, small comfort
in her hand that warms itself all over
minutes off in the next room.

No one so fond of geese and the unmarred sky
could ignore this frame house
defiant in new cold. I believe the white-tailed deer
begin to forage, packs of strays
among the catkins and viburnum
begin their own motifs of forage
beyond our mildewed stumps.

Deeply scarred by things come out of weather,
orange fall of marigold,
bright coins let roll until pin-small
they disappear in the old grass:
my close hours are like low trump,
sixes and fives let go though with reluctance,
by a man called to interpret
the crow's feet and the smile lines,
the passage of the snow geese
he might build faiths on.

Sundays in Parish Neighborhoods

I was too thin for belts, in blue suspenders,
unaware of my own body as nostalgia,
the larger bodies of my family like a fascinating cirrus
I enjoined at such a vantage.
My grandfather, for instance, and for reasons
he never told us, turned late to canvas,
to the inch-tall jars of colors in his study,
until his hand would not stop trembling,
perilously abstract.

I was 7, on Sundays visiting
my grandparents after Mass, waking
the drunk uncles that lived in both their houses.
I remember my grandfather at his table,
over his easel in hard light. But heredity shears,
disavows as it seeks level, makes a new kind
out of the influences I've supposed, my mother's
father, those uncles in whose eyes I took on
a significance, bachelor accountant and custodian
keeping their ledgers and graves clean.

Maybe for all the paintings I came into,
in leather ovals, on charcoal or brown mattings,
it's their voices I keep still, completing
the dark October Sundays, like those of men
encouraging other men to wager. . .

Whatever I understood of provenance,
like whispers over a child still not wakened,
was so exactly borne by landscape, the block
around that building, the bitch in the next flat,
obedient to litter. Going back is one way,
and absence one, to understand perimeters, the way
old men will come to the same corner
after their bus has been re-routed, or men
will go on talking, sink into their arm chairs,

but talk reservedly, as if their tables
and their chairs were in other places yesterday,
with no plot, no compensations to field
as promises, without a child to convince them,
by his faith, of their safekeeping,
but wrapped in his own conceptions of a Sunday,
the rooms brighter than they were ever,
and the block snowed in.

My Grandparents' Dance

The blue morning prepares a cold noon.
I stare, blink clear. The dining bay
and window seat. Triangles of leaded glass
make diamonds in the upper small-paned
windows allowing light.

Shadows of birds through double glass
cross watery over hardwood.

                                        And in Twenties
double parlors, the woodwork imitates
the past century's elegance. My grandparents
dance to scratchy gramaphone recordings,
in these rooms dance to static broadcasts
on a large-dialed transcontinental radio,
are drawn back, then toward one another,
their halt-step surviving from Napoleon and Bismarck
like dyed crosses and spiked pates.

My grandparents' ordinary whispers
stand rockface, static, their common dance,
that particular lovely body's
pressure along his thighs. The water
was not so cold they could not adjust.
The salt was not so unpleasant
they stayed out.

In Flood Country

From rolled wood blinds
            they peered down off porches,
under skies livid with rust
            peered down. The marble christ,

my grandfathers told me,
            cracked at its base
and weather-streaked, rose
            into a changed sky

off the weed and gravel shoulder.
            Houses dropped like miracles
out of our family. That true glass
            the coalstove fire warped

I've kept these years
            to hold me at my temper. . . .
Deaths we presumed worked out.
            New fat christs appeared,

on the lawns, the dashboards,
            in creches beneath
splotched elms, under flaming tents.
            1946 through '54,

twenty-five buck flat,
            my father stoking coalfires
in a low cellar after dark,
            carrying ashpans out to sheds

a decade's winters would pull down.
            That history, never mine
exactly, explains things finally,
            cessation of snow

on a day in April, change of snow
        to rain. Walls of water,
of mud, plow the houses down. And
        my father, our landlady's

errand boy and nightfire,
        bears that scar still, welt line
from just under his thumb to wrist,
        where the ashpan burnt him,

the sounds of cold water
        that panicked surly men to tears. . . .
Tonight, a cool wind
        lifts off quiet water,

out of mixed grain rolls
        the troubled nervures of the world.
Saviors, good jokes
        told badly, play cards

around scratched tables
        talking to their thumbs,
the same half-told stories
        of knee-deep mud and sandbags,

the same omissions like ellipses
        where the water
stored their lives.

First Confessions

After the practices, the iced lime drinks
in my best friend's lower flat,
I talked myself through it, clumsily,
like a sky I still remember, sprawling
but without much light, then brightening,
a contradicting evidence I weighed
against myself. Silver-green leaves stand out
against the lower darker foliage.
Marked as they are by wind, they are
the backs of hands moving over prayer beads,
the dexterity of older women
at the corners or at the window seats. . . .
My eyes shut fast in that rectangular dark,
I spoke of the past week, events
like flakes of almond blown up through light
behind my eyes, terrors my prayers
could not obscure. And none of them said
so what, the kindly inept men
who heard me at confession, never dismissed
the magazines, the palm-sex an older boy
took time to number, none of them
said *so what,* stopped short a boy's enthrallment
with catastrophe. I expected silence,
murmurs, the tics of laughter I got used to,
and Saturdays on the back porch
repeating penances, each prayer distracted
invalidated and resaid, one prayer
thirty times, one more than that even. . .
The street names read like histories,
the house numbers codes, the older homes
of the Italians who would not sell out,
filled with crucifixes and madonnas. Today,
I confess my griefs to God, in wind,
on the same streets and under the signs
of renovation. The point of their endurance
I missed then, hoping to entrap my God,
catching my stumbling too much, looking

for perfect health like a reliable appliance.
The several porches arrayed sidelong
against irascible city winds, their bamboo
shades rolled down like eyelids still,
they seem to squint at the confusion
I could not sort, in the alternating
grey and brilliance, closing but
without strain, to keep dust out
and too much light.

Afternoon Movies at the Catholic Grade School

After the flying saints, the saints
that joked while roasting, there was
nothing we could do. The Mavericks
paled in their flush and shadow,
Space Patrol and Disney paled. There
were flowers wrapped in skirts
where bread was, flowers raining out
of heaven, explaining us, sleeved aces
the Lord tossed down on His gameboard,
backed by His providential grin.
The large grease-stained bags of popcorn
brought from home reminded us
of robes saints sweated their prayers into,
all of us sweating, in unison,
our own decathalons of guilt, punctuated
by bags turned silver in film light.
Then the odds broke down, irregular,
disallowed. And today it's angels,
taking go-carts out for spins they bargained for,
untouchable so long even the Lord
thought them entitled, their looks
like anyone's fallen from such orbits,
drying their lives out. The old
films crackled Fatima and Lourdes,
and men down off their mounts,
equestrian the last time, sharing
their lot with angels. They blame
Christ for showing off, for quitting
early, smiling when they say it,
angels too fond of place, dumb maybe
but well-intentioned, sent out now
to police the quiet side streets,
their ordinary shoulders leaning
earthward, propped on green
flecked posts.

Homecoming

For some reason it's always fall.
Maple and elm leaves raked
in unstable hills. And the leaves
on fire. And the smell
of gutters when the leaves stop up
the sewers after rain.

In fall men warm themselves
in turning leaflight over barrels.
And at forge, foundry, press
and mattress plant, hands at work
turn lightning.

                    My old man examines
shoes he cannot bend down
to polish. He stamps through spots
of time, boy nobody owns up to,
out his front door to smoky corners,
younger and tougher in his versions,
a moon of that true violence
men raise against a city.

We talk. I'm fourteen.
His tumbler's filled with whiskey
on the white stool beside his bath,
the mirrors steamed, water sloshing
as he pulls his legs up
to his chest, spine and mortgage
paid for keeps.

                    We drive at night
through town, through
this city raised up some place
between slobbering and Marx,

our little faith a touring car
in smoky light, wreck of suspensions
on wrecked streets stinking
of sealers and blacktop.

The plant sleeps standing
where I leave him, its thousand eyes
wide open, facets of light,
corrected, that men made lives of.
I drive home without a permit
in a car as still as death, down streets
where my friends cling, where
my friends leave to marksmanship
and pacts and minted breath,
through blocks I practiced
not to love.

DAUGHTER OF THE EMPIRE

Daughter of the Empire

The rules of ceremony relaxed, told
		in a diary made public. The youngest
is pregnant with the first
		of her four children, a fact she finds
no honor in, as she finds no honor
		in her brothers' words about their father,
about their youngest brother's troubles.
		She trusts the future regards them cruelly,
appraises their enemies with a trust
		she has felt for them against her brothers.
His voice comes back to her tonight,
		a remark he made about the age they
settled into, that party gone out to snow,
		to the horse-drawn sleighs
where they imitate their fathers, themselves
		as they might have played as children.
She sits at table sketching, circles
		over circles, skaters and skaters' faces,
couples walking along a boardwalk
		out of the winter they would pardon.
Her hand picks up the same slow drift
		across an oil-smoothed thigh or forearm,
over the belly the neighbor wives
		have not raised to gossip yet. Woman
with a code more private than the country's,
		taken by the scents of cinnamon
and rosehips, she turns so in hall light,
		where the hanging planters menace,
fierce birds scissoring that turn
		of flame and shadow, the brandy lit
on the last of their plum pudding, turns,
		in that fire of plurals men slide into
when standing apart becomes so frightening
		they give themselves to praise.
She settles into her future, seen now
		as the shapes of bones she held above

that fire, brittleness she adjusts to
            in advance, in her homemade blouse
frayed at the cuffs and at the elbows,
            the pearled, gold-clasped barrette
holding her hair back
            until the ceremony's finished.

Reflections on Her Father

Twelve blocks at ten below. The snow
drifting where she walks, more dangerous
this Sunday after dark, traffic
routed elsewhere, a slow pulse on the causeway
north out of the city. She tugs
her hood close, allows the fur-lined slit
she sees through, assured this cold
is discomfort, not jeopardy, as she returns
through backyards, the snow reminding her
of names she and her brother shared as children.
She remembers the sofa, stuffing pushed
through ripped upholstery, the loft in the carbarn
they leapt from to that sofa, the bodies
of children smudging air like local ways
of speaking. Winter branches recall the lines
of argument, of accent, a woman approaching
her with grain, but the weather holds her back,
gone now slowly, disappeared as down
a porch stoop into blizzard. The snow,
sifting off the branches, blown, seems
lit by an enduring she can't fathom, as a gas say,
revolving, grown luminous with its own
motion. And the others, at their windows,
lose their distinction as the cold clouds
their heavy afterdinner breathing. She
sees them now, the crosscuts all scarred over,
and for all she knows the horses
may still dream thaw as an event, a man
bearing the grain out for a woman
to the horses he could not love.

Women Drinking Beer

After Manet

I imagine what words catch in their throats,
angle as light angles. They stop twice weekly,
drink their beer, not so old they must decline light,
so young they need to worry about the barley
at their hearts. Still tight-waisted, with assistance,
still attractive at their breasts: they set
my afternoon to order, in their similar browns
and blues, women so nearly sisters
in their dark round hats, this one hunched over her hand
turned grave, fist almost squeezing the air out,
this other drinking, her fingers lit with amber
through her tilted glass. They are my excuse,
these women, their sisterhood at the edge of its collapse,
bored with affairs, with children. Mademoiselle
will not drink. She will not look up
to light. I hold my place in this foreground beyond
their bows and rings, beyond accoutrements
turned grave. I see them posed so long I cannot
rescue them from color. Somewhere our stories
inevitably collide, splinters like hail through yellow light
fanned through a strange air. And somewhere
a variation commemorates this pair. There is
an owl seen in the long mirror over her piano,
censor, brother, husband, its pinch no longer
painful at her shoulders, its dark eyes gazing
over the snows of petticoats, winters
of chemisette.

Married Mother Out of Her Profession

The women upstairs leave fashionably
at half-past eight. The morning whines
my daughter's rough tugging at its seams.
Odds are a life of sympathetic business.
And odds are a second birth.

The secretaries, come home back up
the drive, theirs is an envy without
regrets, their complaints mine once,
job griefs of single women, a woman
in one room sweating over dinner
on a hot plate.

And some nights,
in the quiet after nursing,
I distract myself so on my daughter's
yellow shoebox, attach such criminal
imaginings to that box, in which whole
trains of husbands will be scattered,
small faces will survive in a warm
though wild climate.

But when she cries out, and when
I find her, secure now in her dreams,
fist closed around her blanket,
her mouth secure around the anchor
of her thumb, I forgive us our
half-intentioned play by which she's present,
the man bearable, bearable that share
of dependence at my breasts.

When I return he's full of sleep
I guess, back arched toward me,
face to the far wall. I cannot explain
what my heart feels toward that body,
toward my daughter, whose increasing
agility instills such fear.

Rather, it's my eye imposing such
resemblance on *her* face, that sees
my gestures in her own, it's the pleasure
in that rub, that helplessness
involves so, starts this thrum across
the table in rhythms wholly foreign,
fixes this life I build around her
that she must see come down.

Sister Margaret/Sgt. Anne Barnes

Based on a newspaper report about a nun who, after years of work with juvenile delinquent girls, left her order to join the vice-squad of a large city police force. She reviews her life, the two decades from age twelve, its two careers grotesquely counterpointing one another.

The bishop's swat confirmed these legs
curled under me, these hips, this handbag,
change of garb expecting breasts,
as if the cloth and cord, the coarse tailoring
of novitiates, took origin from his palm
raised to condemn or promise.

I marked how the leaves put on their gaud
at the first cold. The branches flared.
More consummate than wildfire,
reduced to privacies and closets, women flared,
flaunting bruise and wardrobe, like
filters through which scenes pass,

inducted by blood for keeps. Here
were the notes, the quarter-notes, dance
and deadfloat of humanity down in its cups,
these women, like figures in films slowed
from blurs to stills, their taut calves
practiced for descent,

the brick walls spread to sesames
before their patrons. Now this young woman's
rough hand covers my own. I study
her scars, her calligraphy of nightmares.
This woman, she is the ocean walking upright.
This is her face the artist

cannot settle on the canvas. This is her face
that resists through its dramatic changes,
like stark light transformed dull
between the ledges and the windows, as if
someone raised the veil and tampered
with her smile. I choose,

deliberate. I thrust my hands, palms up,
in front of you, beckon your skin,
your talisman. For you, Sir, the blessed water
burns. For you, the passage stirs
with sirens. But nothing deters, detains.
Nothing is replayed but the count,

the language of bargains and hard sells,
where the priest even, compelled
by the priestess, yields, turned
by her lyre and her silks.

The Patriarch with No Sons Left

Snow foot-deep through connecting yards,
the fences blown or plowed down.
Sub-zero sunlight. Bodies I cannot give up
complicate. A woman turning off
her faucet, frying breakfast steaks and eggs.
A father teaching his son lessons
he will teach to his own son, in a language
he has not learned yet.

Events possess my blood, painted-over
mirror, its beds and chairs, its wrought
dressers part of a larger formlessness,
in which mud-sloshed streets spill down
to cots beside the ocean, in which
I enter and draw back.

A thing feminine starts these spasms
up my spine, delicate as milkweed
blown over asphalt, the body's fine couplings
as delicate as plants stirred up
by wind. They are subject, transparencies
only visible in certain light, the gymnast,
the woman selling ice-cream on the boardwalk,
blonde four years my junior, their children
like pictures turned up in a well-read book,
but I can't say: I rant, conduct my rummage,
I bear my sadness the pictures
cannot touch on.

I read these odd double-person notes,
the last ambitions smeared. They foster
confusion as a man would sons. And still,
the weather-fixed exteriors. And still,
the wooden grip at my right side. I walk
as though snowblind through my rooms,
listen to the morning traffic spin its rough glyph.

Once, light entering tall grass
just off a highway in the north, the air
thick as it was summer, I saw my
shoulders, elbows, wrists all going back
to water, all except that hand bearing
my weight against sure fall.

The Patriarch's Last Days

Night, sludge backdrop to century-old trees,
Men in boots, in wide-brimmed brown and ox-blood
leather hats. The traffic has been silent
how long, the small repeating grotesques silent?
The weather is lost, half the sky blown away.

A belligerent grandfather scraping carrots
spits into the white porcelain jar
beside his straight-backed chair, his chair
tilted out of light against the wainscoting
of his kitchen: means a granddaughter turned bad,
a grandson: spit, and execration. . . .

He misunderstands the cant of their glazed star. . . .

And she, beyond his luxurious glassed gardens,
repose of stone, tiles, and orderly fenestrations,
woman extravagant with her hair pulled back,
calling to a young man across the hedge-row,
or his grandson leaning across the parapet

with cherries: So Polis becomes acceptable,
improvisation of men forced by history
to travel, the sere caravans, the night-ringing
fires, become post-boxes and curbed streets
to spite a past of confiscation. . . .

Stone-like centuries at his heart, it pleases:

How wide his arms sweep, how near his embrace,
hyperborean his breath. His sentries
exact such tribute where they pass. Backs hunched
to a continuous music, likelihoods
on board stairs: theirs is this fever, torque,
this exaggerated ugliness and veneration,
his lush confused findings, piss down a thigh
he cannot get over, absinthe
he cannot forgive.

In the Back House

1

White drapes. Gold tasseled cords
holding the drapes wide. A few stars appear
after rain, over the side porch,
sun parlor. The tall fine-drawn amethyst vase
glows purple in close light. The point's
assembly, these drilled strung shells, reminders
of Bar Harbor and neighbor parts, whatever
sense works up from detail, the imitation chain-lit candles,
the oval needlepoint under glass
in maple frames, delivering me from them, Andrew,
George, William, three brothers I remember
in cuffs rolled twice. In this back building,
on these boards where I look across
the washed blue spindle rail, I correct that now,
bless the city-hired clean up of the house
they let me manage. Balled down, jimmied down
by muscular tanned men, the woodwork
that affects another continent scavenged out in pick-ups,
there, in the house I could not live in,
in the deep-drawered, walnut, hand-ornamented
sideboard, there the narratives collapse,
the memories of our father like knuckles
swollen after brawling, faces, whole bodies
fallen into trances, into dance steps. . . .

2

The unlit candles, washed crystal,
what happened there, the fruit baskets
and the thimbles connecting me
to Europe, I correct that now, left to fragrances,
to dinner stories like unmentionable
thin soups, to the style of a father
whose Christmas became his children's.
I have no doubts about their deaths,
fit to this century, and I do not doubt
my death, so benignly startling
I will pick up half-sentence into reflex.
But that's no answer in itself, nor
these transoms I've looked over into rooms
closed off. And so the house comes down,
the rain pooling in the nightstand's lower drawers,
as if the rain could be concerned
about their sporting caps and monograms!
I trust my body to go on reckoning
given time, despite the cold's history
of knuckles, less a strangeness
I take for granted, all its pensivity
a kind of dance traced back to pollen.
I work out my bad dreams toward a different kind
of spring. My thin-stockinged feet
course these fire-warmed planed boards,
removed a bit from the divining
we put our bones to.

Woman Without Sons

There are times I think *stay put*
Then light on the burnt orange draperies
calls up mornings like my own,
only years from now, and I'm not here,
in this house nursed to the conclusions
of a mortgage, not anywhere really, though
measures I've lived to get here, they endure.
Faces from the past light up
like happy evidence, history cancelling *that.*
And on those days I walk down
the elm-lined sheltered streets, to the park
where my sons played with the children
who outgrew them. One age rushes toward another,
I've supposed. Like tiger bones
raised up from pits that fooled the tiger.
Like this complicated music fingers
like my own could not accomplish. The wind
is still warm though the sky's been dark
for hours. And through bamboo shades
the dark is rhetoric, sufficient enough
to draw us to adagios to come. The driftwood
may as well be a new world. The run
of 8th notes on a fingerboard some kid
has reinvented. Their voices drift up to me
through the dark leaves, come up
front stairs through doors the past
has blown open, effective celebrations,
accordances that will not give them time
to find a mother: this one's bruised hands'
recovery of arbors. And this one,
with stories he remembers but will not tell me,
balanced now on wire I would not dare
over water shuffled white, over the rocks
like chorus lines decked out
in their cream skirts.

Stage Fright

Her face opens into song,
a virtual image she remembers
from which the morning takes its cue.
A look east, glance into ochre,
the deep blues of a mortality
she bears too avidly for grace.
She looks out through damaged blinds,
her mind on storks and river sallows,
black-stockinged chanteuse,
her desire turned to scenes
she remembers after winter,
of children dropping off their 2nd story porches,
unharmed to the plowed snow.
She looks back into her parlor,
the blue walls and the grey
baseboards, the grey door frames,
the blue-grey pile carpet.
And that winter, deeply guarded secret,
a fabric pinned and cut to pattern,
takes its shape beneath her
automatic fingers.

Then sun, then heat she's
almost ready for, bent low,
as she scoops a few leaves off
her balcony's strewn floor,
that have rested out their winter.
She tosses the leaves up, no
pretense of metaphor to save them,
no windy guarantees she might
mistake for sense.

And the sun, magisterial in collapse,
yields this El Greco aftermath
of twilight, the next day's weather
like wooden chips she pieces,
her own day viewed now as a woodcut,

not for stars signalling cool dawn,
not for the last freight or mail plane
lost as it rose off the horizon.

But for something then.
Maybe the face on the scapular
she half-invents, brown-toned
postage stamp of grace,
for the human fly she wept for
in the morning press, having
fingered and toed to the 3rd story,
nothing but sky after
and the long climb down.

Heat Wave

An intermittent though dry wind
lifts candy wrappers and advertisements
around her as she walks.
The night is not long off.
And endurance, after such heat,
studied to a throb of blood,
is sufficient in excess of events,
rendezvous by day in one-story taverns
over cold beer and patrons
unashamed of sweat.

Her fingers idle her loose string tie,
slip occasionally over the eagle clasp
into her half-open blouse, purple fade
of skirt. She half-wishes epiphanies,
assignations, something that though thin
would surprise her, holding back the fire
when she presented it to light.

By now they would speak sensibly,
negotiate their cold. But she goes
through streets unfanned, without
the iced lime drinks, the small necessities
of their moment, ornament off balance
on her blown chrome twig.

She clears her throat to sing,
thinks better of the lyric, withdraws
her own hand now outside
the city's gate, her fervor become
such boredom, that requires something
in the night so like a woman's voice
though it is not that quite.

THE LINDBERG HALF-CENTURY

The Baby Sitter

Our brother told us right, high priest
of drawers we hushed over, pilgrims stopped
by relic pieces. Nights they left us
in his care, the four of us watched transfixed,
Europe saved like coins in a knotted
olive stocking, and under the boxer shorts
in leather albums we were not allowed to touch,
and under the albums in the uniforms
folded in place more than a decade. Then Lebanon
erupted. Then uniformed men at the greased gates,
working fountains like ironies behind them.

And the pictures of our brother mailed back,
reconnaissance filling out his letters, scouting
for evidence of fires, for smoke in the wide beds
of the thistle, for small furred bodies
like pulse points on the earth. The mind plunges,
no silk to hold it back, out of a sky grown
careless, chemical, in the little after sunlight.
Germany, not Lebanon. The last letter arrived
from Athens, news of earth tremors, judgments.
I see him there, the nursed metaxa on his table,
in the same light half a generation quit,
quitting Asia, something troubling him still
about the scenes he cheapened for our sakes.

The four of us come in after an afternoon
near 80. Then the spread of color, child's
sense of color, starts this avalanche, or something,
a leaf or mothwing, a petal dropping off
the bottom of a cup, in which we see him, as a form
seen through centuries-old paint, a succession
of overlays we've hoarded.

The letters, like beds threatening to collapse
on their loose slats, quit finally,
in the marrow where pain's stored, parables told

in signs, in silence, the nightmares
he called up pillaging his daylight. He inhabits
an oblivion Time drops, our memories of him
clashing, like stage curtains and bargain carpets
in schools the Church shuts down, his stories
chief of our day's effects, the carnage he designed
to frighten us to sleep spoken plainly now,
with none of the panic of a man afraid
to be found lovely.

Reunion Stills

Fresh from its chemical bath, the first,
clipped to a span of basement wire.

She looks out in a second toward negative breakers.
In her right hand a megaphone. And

in unshaded light illumining a finished still
her face floats, in its wash fixed

on a man who bears a camera. What grace there is
in the Atlantic's formal cold, less heart

than elegance, is appointed as stills are,
marked, sent out to honor contracts,

one man's clumsy barter, in which her left hand,
held as in dance or in regard, waves home

husband, brother, while the woman glances right
as to a friend or lover. Routine

repeats the nearly perfect angles of her face,
under the brown small-brimmed hat, over

the trenchcoat's collar gathered to her throat.
— Late afternoon, his clustered backland birch

waiting the moon come full. Names like *Rhoads,*
Hinton, Breese, and *Read,* their women,

photographed in blue wool, tweed, fire-sale leathers,
in that wash fixed, in part a mimesis

of time through time, their moment now an axle
set turning in the rain. The photographer

clambers his steep hill, imagines the outlaws
at its crest, figures trading snapshots

of their wives and children. Her own sublime children
are by now entering their women, like men

entering a mirror. And her husband, his companions,
in their strengths as delicate as doilies

or caged birds, curios stopped in the damp wind,
figures locked in sepia the next century

could not afford: they are set, as he is set,
revenant, having ridden the cold homely

into small regard.

Talking It Out with the First Son

Colored slits let day into the stone
lower room. I touched the burning stick
to candles. What originated there,
in that damp room, was not clear cut,
not jeopardy, where I saw myself,
as in a crossview, in a shyness the grotto formed around
against a century stirred up. Except
for early sun, the hand as if on fire
on the pillow, I can't remember any of it
exactly, the last of wine, uncorked,
climbing the still air. I listened
to my voice, trying out the inscriptions
in the hymnal, fixed against
an uninvited party. The shifting plates
of memory
heat through to combustion. And for
all that talk of birthdates and intentions,
ice chips shifting against the false
bottom of their wagon, the past, returned
as up an airshaft, race of cold flames,
a man hidden under ice and fish in a wood cart,
smuggled across a checkpoint, the past
was nothing like the getaway old films
tell, the puzzling spokes racing back
into lives nobody trusted. . . .

Only something holds, the moon, the lake
and something, her tongue and mine,
that she drew back from into her handbound
book of sketches, the last night
at the back rail, our fingers almost touching,
relaxing, releasing, on that rail
they do not hold exactly, do not forget.
We both knew what we meant, lovers,
not dead but subject, inhabiting a building
put up wrong. She goes barefooted

down the concrete steps to puddles, avoiding
the broken glass as she is able,
multiplied, as a figure seen on mirrors,
a repeating locus at the fringe of her
vocation against the State. We both knew what
we meant. Not what anybody maneuvering
the expressway could have figured, looking up
for the full moon after rain. Not whatever
among the nightsearched stars struck,
seeding our pasts with arson.

Custodian at His Window

A mean field of sight opens.
Over railings brutalized by mopsticks
light tears into, sharpens
his patch of furnished room. He is
the spokesman for this cold.
He listens to the birds of fresh snow,
men compelled to shovel out,
the vibrating, persistent songs
that bear the right words up.
Later, the sky greys up for storm,
the second since Thanksgiving.
He marks how the cold-furrowed expressions
clamp, release. A knobbed boot
drives a red blade deep to blacktop.
And the boys, their exposed
cheeks taut, throw snowballs in the street
beyond the black wrought-iron
fencing: *his odd catch at such*
a window: the frayed ropes he must
replace, the repaired frames
and rebuilt casings, barbed wire
secured to granite posts
that marks his employment from their own,
the concrete block apartments,
their red framed windows vivid
against grey stone, through
walls of blown snow. The curriers
from the neighborhood come late,
displaying the photographs, the bold-
faced aliases he goes by. A man
will ravage his own sons, his thought
a weathering orange complement
to frost. A man will convene along
the rafters with his angels,
their expressions like blown
strands of light becoming solid,

fetching his confusion, figures
frozen to a lawn scene, of boys,
swords, barreltop shields, a boy
that stands apart who would be
hacking down a snowman, his shovel
opening the head of a boy
who steps between.

Turncoat

Based on the legend of the stone mason, about to be martyred, who denied his Christian faith, saving his life, who was in that moment condemned to life without death, until he would have his chance to testify again to his faith at Armageddon.

Not inclined to sleep, not fully awake either,
I fall through morning, as a boy
straying off a dock will fall through water,
remembering the darkening guardian light,

the cold his body surfaced out of,
years after the event. My future rigged to no
sure place, I watch my daughter, how many
daughters before this, struck by her thinking,

not yet three, at martyrdoms men perfect.
Men grave with convenience linger, repeating
words like *casualty* and *curfew*, and local wars
gutter the cities of the world. Still,

it's them I hear, in their deaths, the first to die
for Christ, not praising the Father
as I guessed, but crying out as the paw crushed,
marked them for the next age. I wasn't

alone backing out, unburned, untorn, my faith nothing,
not like theirs anyway, nor was I the last
to reason a pardon I could trust. But even the Twelve
fled, flinched, all before the flex

of Resurrection, and they were present then,
save one, eyewitnessing that changed man
in the midst of things. Each day the world's bared,
opened like his back, man taken into custody

for treason. Each day the world repeats,
assurances of men who pay their memberships
on credit. How do you protect a child from that?
Plenty may be as threatening

as the short barrel of a pistol, no less real,
    as I go on about this fate, again and again
failing, struck by the maroon question marks
    on white fields, the ironies of certain intersections

where I have learned the terrain and language.
    But my body was no torch, no bait,
I told myself, mistaken as I saw it, a measure dropping
    deeper in the face of lesser threats.

I cannot forget the grown children circled
    by the fire, forget the gun-powder's punctuation,
drowning the whimpers of the heretic, whimpers
    given to screams. I go on,

a posted guard condemned to notice.
    I watch the duets of earnest men,
that man's head blown open for the newsmen,
    whose eyes never left my own.

In a Late Hour

Those days the day-gang ravaged gallons
on the burnt slope below the highschool,
stumbled Mary Street downhill to Lodi.
There was no work. Boys not so inclined
stayed on anyway, got schooled in time
for Europe, left a city
full of breweries, came home to families
believing their wars done. That stretch
of shade trees was the only fencing
when he started, spotty enough now to hint
the details of a texture. The wrens
did celebrate that year. And those
trees now, like excerpts, preserve still in italics
among the brick and restored cobbles
a testament skies gather,
how there never was more chance. There is
convenience in the clean lines at the edges
of his dark, the bush and gates
and awnings running the edge of his cold sky.
He listens to that dark, drawn out
from reasonable ceilings down the sluice
of an old year, into the wheels
of smoke, the spokes of lean birch, listens
to limbs advancing snow across
the snow-caved roofs. Time of small beer,
hands that drift in and out of fire,
casual risk. The trucks drift still out
48, some trees left, some decades old,
bone hard. He has lived anxious
in one place even flames refused, come
unblistered home. Now his hands
turn fires he cannot deny.

Jesus in the Tomb

After reading John on Good Friday,
consoling a friend at a topless restaurant.

The rending ceased, monitors of caved gut,
drilled anklebones and wrists diamonded by pain,
then the pain quit. Their spices, windings,

their proportioned hands dedicated as angels'
in Your service, that one dark passage behind stone razed
in a single brilliant instant. Good Friday,

I read John, console one sad man. I think
of Your wounds gradually perfected. But today
I am too much skin. Today a stranger's breasts

seem nearly muscular curling up below her nipples.
How many flexed that stone in place? And how
many bored beyond event or pleasure woke fortunately

to glimpse what they never could explain? Pain
no longer possible, the dank air commemorative
with voices, was that second Nativity

all that You expected? I watch her move, study
her posture against a bank of air. And here,
on this cold floor significant with distance,

I think of Your gesture breaking the rhetoric of morning,
Your passage like a cipher through peelings
of stone and space. Were the women's hands

transfigured in Your presence? And this daughter
at her fortune like blown brush, are her hands
transfigured ever? We stand this blemish

on our affection, the exposure and the dance
and the premeditated blush, remember the second
mother taken in one man's version

the while one performs to call, Your Passion intervening as through hollow doors, letting enough of sentence in.

The Lindbergh Half-Century

Based on a newspaper report regarding a man in Buffalo N.Y. who discovered, upon reading *The Buffalo Evening News* commemorative reprint of its announcements on Lindbergh's arrival in France, that his mother, who according to his father and grandmother had abandoned the family when she went out to buy him ice cream, had actually been beaten and strangled, dumped in Ellicott Creek, that his father had been implicated or at least questioned by the police. I tried to imagine his shock, having probably played and replayed scenarios of her aging and dying through those five decades, to discover the facts behind her death, how the revelations might have caused him to reassess his life, his achievements and tragedies as well as those of the nation's hero.

The roads to Buffalo in winter
were clogged, impassable,
the city and canal locked with ice
that ran traders' blood
through the Mohawk to the Hudson.
1927, a century on water finished.
Rails, some planes, trucks,
the city sprawling suburbs,
pre-Depression Upstate, the Twenties,
the tightbrowed, iced, Upstate
flatlands waiting through winter
for heroics. My mother leaves,
I'm three. Fifty winters back,
trudging knee-deep drifts, the city
welcomed spring, and *Lindbergh*
In France, breaking winter's
isolation of coastlines and slow boards.
My mother leaves to buy me
ice cream. She does not come back.
Lindy's crossing caps a dry
prosperous decade after battles.
Fifty years since, motherless.
She goes to the sheet in mistletoe.
She goes bobbed, bedazzled,
strung beads into the city.
Goes low-heeled in her house-dress.

A ground level wind fascinated
by her garters hints death
and broken lots, trails Lindbergh
through unrelenting sleet,
Lindbergh through his crises,
wind scuffling over stepstones
into dark blocks without
respite. . . .

As if the innumerable dead could not keep a single death
a secret! Tonight, the French coast,

tonight, *The Buffalo Evening News'* pen and ink commemoration
detailing, describing flight. May, 1927.

One item center-left diminished beneath the headlines: *Woman's*
body discovered, strangled, beaten, in Ellicott Creek,

her husband questioned but not charged. That fine print
jolts my guard, the pavement scored by wind and lightning

yawing underfoot. My mother beaten, strangled. The old man
dead. Shed from what tactility our lives afford.

Through the reprisal-lacking lean Thirties she had not reneged
on birth! I think closed rooms. I recall that boy muttering

her coded name, a dream-like investiture, her pictures
fading into pastels. My mother dying, twice!

The death I had imagined, waist-deep in grave grass, and this
dying, before thirty dead, yielding to long snow

and nightshade. Lindbergh's reception was no more foreign!
My grandmother and father, as if some pact were

wrought between them for my sake, silent. Murder reduced to trivia by one man's prowess.

Mute for my sake!

Whatever might have hurt them's
finished. Whatever bound them's
judged. So Lindbergh finessed
weather, taking the French air deep.
No one can say where she is buried,
beneath what maple, dismantled elm
she lies the recipient of what
cleric's token say. I pardon their
benevolence, the old man's guilt
or innocence no matter, find her days
through my own, this accumulating
stock of still-lifes accounting
for her presence. The planet lurches
underfoot. Assassins, kidnapers.
The stark hostile registers
of broken bottles at the neckline.
I adapt, resolve these. The violence
of murder-rape made manageable
by telling, I revise her obituary
(Lindbergh's heroics/tragedies
dwarfed by our parochial griefs),
revise my fictive birthright
in this damp wind commencing
a lavish season.

AFTER SLEDDING

Night Swimming outside Ithaca

After the wine and spaghetti supper
we drove the back streets
overhill to the wood-fringed state road
under no moon and the gathered stars
for a late swim in the back-up reservoir.
We parked, broke road for wood.
Patterns of fern and cedar feathered by our light
hemmed the dirt path
and crickets sentried for small animals
scattered by our passage into brush.
The plank bridge caved from excess earlier
that week. Our casual dangers
magnified on public land, we sidled
its last strong board by flashlight,
marked the old wood fallen, that framed
the zigzag cut up the last hill
that dropped to water.

Making believe, breaking surfaces,
remembering the glacial cracks and silence
that crossed the icing night,
we found no floors, dark swimmers breaking
a reflecting surface with downstrokes
to darker water. The pressure at our ears
or the cold after our feet broke water
struck our language from its warp. . . .

Spurred by stars below the tall stone
rudders of the world, forgetting
how men drown from the tightness in their bodies,
we swam sure center, toward that
opposite bank of trees almost ghostly
in low water, our lives less fragile,
less surreal, like ever-complicating phrases
we passed to one another. . . .

What can't be said holds. Months
later, its vivid gesture, the chance
there is nothing better, tries me. Roads
through cut rock led back
from lowland water, sprawled out of the foothills
into a foreign language, wildernesses
of jays and grackles like negotiations
at their edge. I concede to matter
its staggering short while, concede us,
stippled to a deep canvas among
the furbishings of pine. We have risen,
subject, in widening peripheries,
having drifted crosswise over territories
claimed, taking that civilized
wood to heart.

Montreal, after Two Rains

The old men get even with themselves
on benches in warm light. The apples dazzle us
in cribs at our sight's edge, glazed
with the short hour's rain before the sun came up.
We walk the blocked streets, among
Poles, Slovaks, Greeks, men with dark eyes
prone to worship, unfashionable men at counters
breakfasting late on hard rolls and smoked meat.
A half-hour lapses, some few words in German,
and off in the park morning slides delicately,
as a towel lightly drying hip to calf to ankle,
the thigh raised in such a way a husband
may imagine, to the fountains' gush and fall
among arrays of summer flowers. City,
correspondence working out its forms, where our gaze
prospers: within its fusion of particulars
a small wind gathers: we lunch on Polish sausage,
beer and cabbage soup, admire the ladies
in their dance, the remove of their inflections
like windchimes lifted after rain. Bodies
like flames, engagements! We applaud as kin,
husbands, our hands of builders, tablemakers
settling over heartwood, approving the figures
we are given, their bodies elongated now
as swimmers below the surface of a river,
gentle after rain, after so long heat.

November: Between Riparius and Speculator

On Route 8 southwest of Riparius, N.Y.
I pull off, open my car to snow.

I walk a little past my car. And after
some time, tired of watching water

that has not frozen yet, I walk back,
brush the wet snow off my rust-colored sweater,

lean awhile on my front fender, no
nearer to my life than this mood diffused

in shades of snow and water. Uphill
off the left shoulder, planes of rockface

wet with snow, the darker greens
of conifers reaching up through falling snow

into a thick snow cover, intoned
until my raised arms cannot bear it

any longer, all sensible family grief
and laughter in hues of stone and snow . . .

It will take me ten years to describe it.
Hurried by funeral, by christening,

I looked off from driving, as a man
will look to check a door he believes

he should have bolted, before returning
to his business, to coffee he cannot drink

steaming the heat back through his fingers.
And just past that bridge across

the Hudson a girl on horseback waved.
I skidded left, recovered, paused those

few moments in snow my wheels rutted,
my heart a warning between prescience

and a mind made up, how tired from life
our lives become, how I might

have stayed for days.

Autumn after a Lean Year

Hints of fall in middle August,
the year mounting grey-black clouds
over steet and seaboard,
a mixed fervor, disinclination
in the wind off-pulse. I have
talked windows, talked chairs burnished
in genuine parlors, the hawk-
riddled coastal air, fathered here,
fouled and recovered love.
In the green back bedroom, on cold
nights scribbling, I listened
to boards in storm, the house trying
to keep warm. Hours distilled
to primaries science can't discount.
Say I have lived here sparely,
entered a few lives closely, happened
on a life more quietly my own
than puzzling. The voices of my family
from our common rooms remind me
in this bedroom where I sway for heat.
It was summer, at the edge
of fall, as yet unchanged, two
walking a third in that same light
by which their quarrels cleared.
The year, a light through rye
and ice, flared, as old lights flare
before concluding in mixed dark.
Two, too puzzled to say when.
Then bright water so intimate
two could see to change.

Thanksgiving Weekend: The Last Touch Football for the Twenty-fifth Season

Sunday. Small hammers tapping
the storm-windows into place.
On windy Sundays after Mass, late
August through November,
in sweats, in paint spattered pants,
they drive to the old neighborhood
for football, and after football home
for smoked meats and ale.
Small luck primes them for the kindness
they stray on, their own aches
that remind them of, two decades
earlier, the passes they just missed,
the flying tackles they completed,
bodies sprawled on thorns
where a rose garden lined one drive.
If the attitudes remain, the aversions,
interests, and if the century,
like a running back trying to regain
his balance, stumbles forward
toward the next, their lives take on
the appearance of a truce seen
at a distance. They know to expect
rust. They know an explanation
falsifies events they are a part of.
But here, their pasts spread-eagle
on forever, in tall backed chairs
at walnut table, their lives,
of which they speak as some men
will speak of sandblasting with a reverence,
they give thanks for, in that
wash of scents and water lights
where their beauty is at first
chilling, like that of a family
entering night fog, an unexpected
radiance that becomes a habitation,

men opening in their close company
as an orange grove will seem
to open, without prescience
of frost.

For Matthew Clarkson,
For Luke Moore Clarkson (in Memoriam)

I am dumb to address my Lord
 in His indifferent north.
Late autumn's inviolate cold
 locks fast a man

made vulnerable by warmth.
 Yet all mention of God,
weather, puts off grief,
 a friend's day-old son

dying in New England,
 and this lamp I've turned down
in the event of prayer
 reminds me of his dark,

infatuating, cruel. Matthew,
 your strong browned hands,
attending casket boards, lathed
 and finished rough wood

to crib, cradle, painted
 the wood horse
a small ghost stays on to ride.
 Nobody there could count

the deflections you have
 managed, to sax or keyboard,
to glasses face down in a restaurant
 expecting a dark wine,

remembering the pierce
 of shrill vocables,
the pre-speech crying out
 for winterberry, phlox.

I see that son's entire
        body pleading, requiring
some management of chaos
        in the place he must forsake.

Music, wine, and morning
        ward off dark at length,
the morning glories started
        on a sun porch. Stepstones

descend to a salt spring
        and cold runs fully over land.
Matt, hacked, roughed open
        and laid to public fire,

ill-prepared by stock
        for the faces
you shall muster: depend now
        on caress, father

removed from your first born,
        the instant
of acknowledgment that eases
        what it cannot
make right.

Taking the Tree Down

Fifty degrees in middle February.
The men shield their eyes to light, laugh,
embarrassed a little, but not
as they expected. The mongrel noses
their cuttings and slinks off. On ground,
their four boys, less trusted to climbing
by their mothers, section the first upper limbs
and stuff them in the pick-up. Their fathers
rest, under the aluminum awning, after the ropes,
the chainsaws. They talk out the next
hour's work in Italian and near English.

A wife's voice calls them, half done,
in for coffee, for the muffins and prune bread
she's set cooling.
                                        When I was five, younger,
I watched the city crew take down
the elm in our front yard. I barely
remember that, except for the vague sense
of a boy at the front window
of his shared bedroom, taken by their motion
as the tree came down to stump.

Having more skyline that I needed,
I closed my window then. But this morning,
taken by her thanks, by the complications
of no motive, I watch for them to come out
still, catch myself at my indulgence
for this tree's sake, unlucky enough to root itself
where three yards come together.

Still warm enough with thaw for men
to sit outdoors tonight, they sing,
ache out minor chords across the mandolin's
paired strings, tease the stops
of the recorder. I listen closely to their song,

mark the white shreds grown eerie
in the cold burn of their floodlight.
The northside's seen its share of trees
come down, heard its consolations
of night talk.

                    The voices under awnings
remembering the spindly frames
of restaurants put up with the factories,
the fish fries and nickle beers, remembering
the bars brought down to cinders: something
to figure something by tonight, while the stackfires
appear on the darkening west sky: like
the stone columns of the candle factory
seen as if for the first time; a marriage
say that leaves off half a family;
or a woman in her stone house, her stove
still warm to touch; or these blocks,
grown so familiar she forgets their names,
where the ghosts, fresh dead, would sniff
among the presses, only a decade
or so back.

After Sledding

Late snow settles around the barn
converted to house two families.
Its washed-brown, painted over cranberry
is lovely in this cold
where I imagine stars, a night below zero
promising a deeper cold to follow.
My breath stuns me, the pitch
of snow under me. Once, a young boy
smashing ice off of a chain fence,
up later than I should be, running
through the backlots with a yard
of broken molding, I imagined the cellos,
the violas confounded by that measure.
Taking the shortcut home through Woodlawn,
I watched for dogs, for old men
in paper houses who would be gone
if I checked back. I stopped
to piss behind one marker, wrote my name
in snow on unmarked stone.
I trust him almost, among the shadows
cast by cemetery hedges, his
practice for tonight, rehearsed
as a boy rehearses his first initiation
or friend's birthday, afraid
his gift will not be right. Memory
attempts a present tense. Porch chimes
affect that ice, the shovel jammed
into packed snow, the old man home
from worship his son would not attend.
In ruts, on ice, throwing myself
against my future, stumbling across
the elm strippings the last storm
took apart: I am tempted to snow angels,
I know what to expect: the roads
glazed, iced by toughs to suit their
urgent need for laughter. Tonight,

the wind that seemed a kind of hardware
behind me now, I enter through foyer
and hall to parlor, to the pleasant heat
of shared rooms like a wager
I find no fault in, having come to trust
this north, that urgent need
for laughter, this city barn
and room upstairs where my daughter
dreams tucked in, tired enough
from sledding to sleep
in a strange bed.

A Poem at my Daughter's Third Christmas

A week below zero. The powdery snow
breaks apart no matter how I pack it.
But where Culbert blunt-edges the boulevard,
my neighbor's boys hose snow, their sticks
propped against, their pads hung over
the chain fence their old man raised around the house
after the youngest son turned four.

This morning, two weeks to Christmas,
we put the porch lights up,
the decorations out, that she, surviving us,
might leap clear of the century's
wrong freight. And after, shopping for St. Nicholas,
driving by the highschool, I watched
somebody else's sons at play, their grid-iron
marked in half-foot snow by stumps and paper sacks.

I saw the ruined cardboard sled
on the small hill below their field
and for seconds lapsed, planning in mud,
in snow, with mud-tipped or gloved fingers. . . .
She looks up at me with eyes
I'm stunned, embarrassed by. Whatever
the deliberate readings of night stars,
whatever winter threatens, I watch her dance,
admire her fine-boned grace as she goes on
about her father, about the sheets and snow
and ceiling swirls, the white complexities
of a future she's yet to build.

I know what I've begun, what affections
I have started. Tonight, showing her
the lights outside, the homes like blocky fathers
on their haunches, I understand
these streets, these yards alongside
or out behind old homes, where the children play,

who will spite their premonitions
and play well, their slapshots home or caroming,
until I find her somewhere down my spine,
in origins beyond my own, in something
like a Christmas, in that dream of sleds and fields
beyond the swaybacked saltbox homes,
a woman warming her child after sledding,
the fire drawing her man close.

About Robert Lietz:

Robert Lietz was born in 1946 and lived most of his life in upstate New York. In 1981 he moved to Wyoming and is currently living in western Ohio. His poems have appeared in many journals, including *The Chariton Review, Epoch, The Georgia Review, The Massachusetts Review, The Missouri Review, Poetry, Shenandoah,* and *Tendril.* Mr. Lietz has taught at Syracuse University, the University of Wyoming, and in 1985-86 was Visiting Professor in Creative Writing at Bowling Green State University. Two previous books, *Running in Place* and *At Park and East Division,* were published by L'Epervier Press and a fourth collection, *The Inheritance,* was published by Sandhills Press.